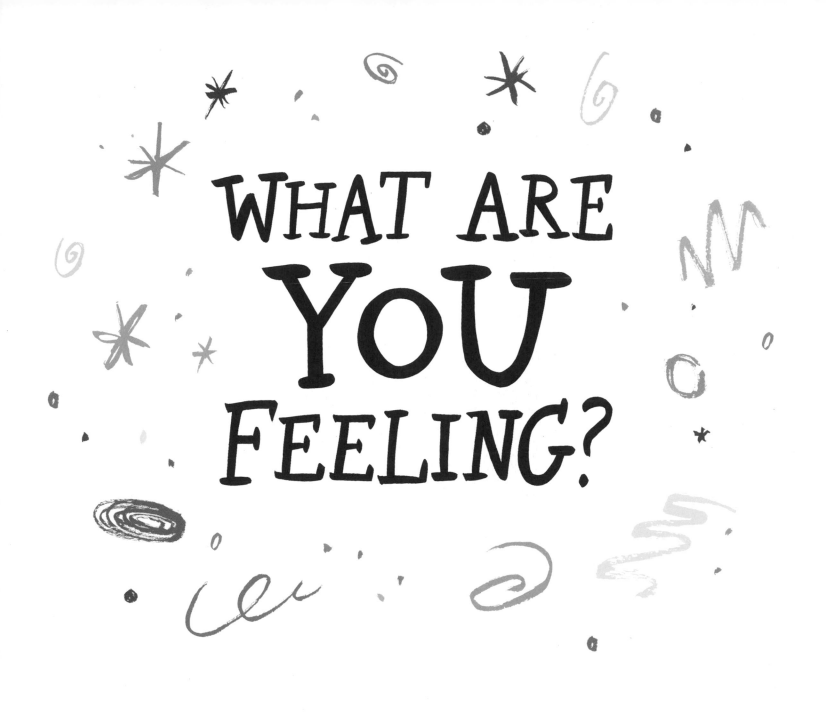

Published in 2023 by The School of Life
930 High Road, London, N12 9RT

Printed in Lithuania by Balto Print

The School of Life publishes a range of books on essential
topics in psychological and emotional life, including
relationships, parenting, friendship, careers and fulfilment.
The aim is always to help us to understand ourselves better
– and thereby to grow calmer, less confused and more
purposeful. Discover our full range of titles, including
books for children, here:
www.theschooloflife.com/books

The School of Life also offers a comprehensive
therapy service, which complements, and draws
upon, our published works:
www.theschooloflife.com/therapy

www.theschooloflife.com

ISBN 978-1-915087-27-0

10 9 8 7 6 5 4 3 2

WHAT ARE YOU FEELING?

The School of Life

Contents

What is this book all about?

Sometimes it's difficult to talk about what you feel

And one last thing ...
What are they feeling?

What *is* this book all about?

Feelings can be complicated, confusing or hard to explain. For example, a cow might have lots of very interesting feelings, but it can be hard to know. You would probably be able to tell from its behaviour if it was *friendly* or *frightened*, but sometimes feelings aren't so obvious, and a cow can't use words to tell you what it's feeling.

You're a bit like a cow. We don't mean that you have four legs and like eating grass! We mean that sometimes it's not obvious how you're feeling. But a great thing about being human is that you can use *words* to *tell* people.

When you were a baby, you couldn't say you were hungry or tired, so grown ups had to guess what you were feeling. But as you've got older, you've learnt to speak. As you grow up, you get more and more complicated feelings. So, it's good to know some more words to help you talk about them.

That's what this book is all about: finding interesting words for interesting feelings. We're going to explore what lots of feeling words really mean and which words best describe the many feelings you may have.

Ready? OK.
But there's one last important thing to say before we start …

Sometimes it's difficult to talk about what you feel

This book is not just about finding the right words to describe your feelings, it's also about helping you to share them with someone else.

The grown-up who reads this book with you is showing you that they want to listen and understand. They're saying that it's good to take time to talk about your feelings *even if they seem very complicated.*

Sharing your feelings is a great way to understand them and to manage them. The person listening to you won't say they're silly or wrong, they'll say something helpful like 'tell me more' or 'it's OK to feel like that'.

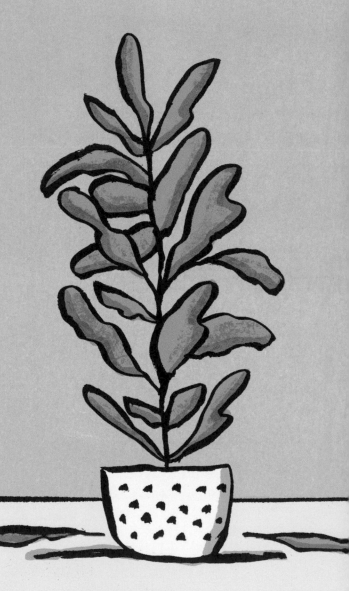

No feelings are bad and
they're always important.
So, let's start talking about
some *interesting feelings*.

Sad

Sometimes it's really tricky to talk about feeling sad. You have a heavy feeling inside. You might want to cry. Your best friend is playing with someone else and you feel left out. Or you just woke up feeling this way and don't know why. Maybe you're sad about something that happened a while ago and it just popped into your head.

This might sound really odd, but it's actually helpful to feel sad. You feel sad because something upsetting has happened. The problem comes if you try too hard to stop yourself feeling sad. You might say you don't care or you don't mind, but inside the sadness is still there.

What sadness needs is someone who understands. You don't always want someone to say, 'Don't worry, it doesn't matter', you want them to say, 'I understand, it's OK to feel sad.'

Silly

It's wonderful to feel silly sometimes.
What if you put your clothes on upside
down? And wore gloves on your feet?
Or pretended the house was upside
down and you were walking on the
ceiling? What if children were in
charge of the world and grown-ups
had to do what you told them?

Silly means having fun with an idea. You're really asking: what if things were different? Silly is when you stop thinking, for a moment, about how things actually *are* and imagine how they *could* be.

Suppose that children taught teachers. That is silly – but also very interesting. What would you teach them? Not maths (they know that already). Maybe a game or a joke? They might like that!

We know that the Earth is a sphere, but people used to think it was flat, like a pizza! In fact, it was considered *silly* to think it wasn't flat. The first planes, made out of wood, fabric and wire, looked very silly. Sometimes silly is how good things start.

Shy

Feeling shy can be really inconvenient. It is about what you think others might think of you. Someone speaks to you but you can't think of anything to say and you just blush. You're supposed to go up and talk to someone, but it's so terrifying that you want to run away. A lot of people seem pretty frightening.

The beautiful thing about being shy is that you understand other people can be different from you. Maybe they've got a loud voice, or they're wearing very smart clothes, but how much does that *really* tell you about who they are? Other people can seem confident, but they sometimes feel shy as well.

You can't just stop being shy, but you can take tiny steps – though they're big steps for you. You can just say, 'hello'. People might turn out to be much less scary than you think.

Worried

Things can feel very scary but can actually be OK. It could feel terrifying to be on a ship in a storm. The wind is so strong. The waves are crashing all around. The floor is tipping. But for the captain and the crew it isn't such a big deal. They've been in lots of storms before, some much worse than this. They know the ship is actually very strong. It will be rough for a while, but everyone will be OK.

You're stronger than you think – and so is the whole world.

There are things on the news that look very scary. But the news doesn't tell you how many other scary things have *already* happened in history. Human beings are brilliant at coping. We can live with, solve and survive all kinds of difficulties.

Angry

Sometimes, maybe you feel like a volcano ...
If you saw a volcano from the outside, it
might just look like an ordinary mountain.
But inside, the pressure of hot lava builds
up and up until, suddenly, it erupts!

It can be like that when you feel angry. At first you might say things are OK, even though they're not really. While inside you're getting more and more furious.

Then, suddenly, you explode.

Maybe you shout something horrible. Maybe you hit or kick someone (even though you know you shouldn't).

It's not bad or wrong to feel angry. You feel angry because something is upsetting or frustrating you a lot. There's a reason why you feel so angry, but it's good to be able to control the volcano.

If you tell someone you trust that you feel angry – and explain why – it can help to stop the explosion.

Bored

Feeling bored is … *interesting*. That sounds crazy! You don't *like* being bored. Maybe you really want to do something, but you have to wait … and wait … and … wait. Or maybe people keep making you do things you're not interested in. Perhaps it feels like there's nothing interesting for you to do.

The feeling of being bored is actually your brain sending you a message. It's saying: '*I'm important, I can be interested in all sorts of things. Make use of me!*'

You have to wait? Boring! Well, maybe you could be writing a poem in your mind or planning a city on Mars. You have to do your homework when you want to play? Boring! No, that's interesting!

What would you really like to learn? Why don't schools teach that? What might be a good reason for doing the homework anyway? These are big questions for your big brain.

Nothing exciting is happening? You can make exciting things happen in your brain. You can imagine and wonder.

Sensitive

A tricky thing about being sensitive is that some people don't seem to care. You're sensitive when you notice and care about little things. You notice when someone else feels shy. You can tell that someone feels sad, even if they say they're fine. Maybe you see how beautiful the shape of a leaf is or how lovely certain colours look together.

It would be nice if everyone saw and felt what you do. But often they don't seem to be interested in the leaves or the colours. They don't seem to notice (or care) what other people are feeling.

But here's an interesting thought: maybe most people feel sensitive, but some people are frightened. Maybe they don't want anyone to laugh at them, so they never say they care about anything. But they secretly do care.

It's important and brave to let other people know about the little things you notice.

Upset

Sometimes everything just feels like too much and you feel like you can't cope. When something's really upsetting you, it can be tricky to tell other people what's wrong. You want them to understand, but maybe you don't want to have to tell them about it or ask them to help you.

You feel awful and everything seems complicated. Maybe someone wasn't very nice at school and they made a mean comment, but you don't want to explain this.

There's something special about all our brains – including yours. Other people can't see what we're thinking, even when it's so obvious to us, so we need to share how we're feeling so that they can help us.

Proud

You've done something really well, and it's good to know it and to feel it. But it can be tricky to celebrate yourself. Maybe you don't want to show off. You know it's not so nice to boast and brag about how wonderful you are. But there's a very interesting problem that comes from the *opposite* direction: you might be shy about telling people that you've actually done something pretty special.

Being proud means admitting to yourself that you've done something that excites you, and you know it says something good about you. You should feel that sense of pride – it's not the same as being boastful. You don't have to tell *everyone* – the main thing is that *you* know.

It's funny, when you *really* know you've done something well you don't actually need other people to agree. You're proud of yourself, and that's what counts – even if, sometimes, no one else realises.

Hurt

Sometimes your feelings can get so sore. Sometimes other children say things to you that aren't very nice. Maybe they say that your drawing is silly or that your hair looks funny. That's not kind at all.

You *could* get upset but you don't *have* to. Those people aren't trying to help you. They aren't world-experts on drawings or hair (or anything else). They are just being mean and silly when they say those sorts of things.

What's important is what *you* think. You don't have to pay attention to what other people say: you can just get on with being you.

Quiet

Often, noisy people get the most attention. Maybe the things that many other people seem to get excited about don't excite you as much. They want to go to a party or run around all the time, but sometimes maybe you just want to draw or read a book or make a really cool play dough model of a castle.

The best discovery for quiet people is that you don't need others to enjoy what you're doing. You like it anyway, and you don't mind too much if other people don't notice. Feeling quiet often means you want to be by yourself for a bit. And that's OK.

In fact, if you take a look around you might notice a few more people feeling quiet, too. You might not always notice them at first, because they're quiet!

Mischievous

It's interesting to think about squirting cream all over your head, but maybe not such a good idea to actually do it!

A very interesting thing about being human is that our minds are so big. We have lots and lots of mischievous ideas that might not be such good things to *really* do. Like putting a dress on the family dog or staying up all night watching your favourite movie five times.

You can enjoy *imagining* what it would be like to be a pirate but actually *being* a pirate would be a terrible career choice.

That is what's so lovely about imagination: you don't actually have to do something mischievous, you can just think about it. It's great to wonder what it would be like to eat twelve doughnuts in one sitting, but you'd have a very sore tummy if you actually did that!

Sorry

You know that you did the wrong thing. You really weren't very nice. Maybe what you did was a bit unkind. Maybe it was an accident and you didn't even mean it. So, why does it feel so hard to say sorry? Maybe you're ashamed or maybe it's because there's a reason you did what you did. You felt upset, picked on or left out.

You *know* you shouldn't have done what you did, but saying sorry feels like saying, 'I'm just bad.' You want people to understand that you're not a bad person. You're a good person who just did something you wish you hadn't. You want to say, 'I really am sorry, but I need to explain …'

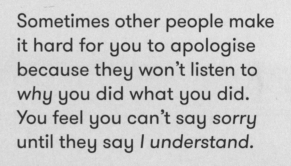

Sometimes other people make it hard for you to apologise because they won't listen to why you did what you did. You feel you can't say *sorry* until they say *I understand*.

Afraid

Different things scare different people. You might be afraid of monsters under the bed or of lions hiding in a cupboard in the kitchen.

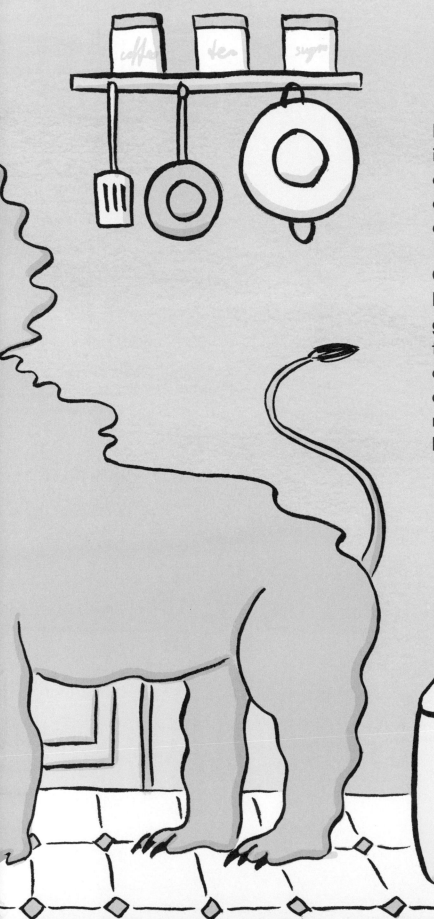

But how would a lion get from the wild into your house? Lions can't drive cars or book plane tickets. If a lion walked down the street in a city, people would call the police.

Occasionally frightening things happen, but most of the time our imaginations get very busy *making up* things to be frightened of. That's why it helps to talk about your fears, so our clever brains can recognise that and say, 'That's not real. It's just made up. It couldn't really happen.' Good old clever brains!

Independent

Sometimes, you're happiest being on your own. It can be so much fun to be with other people, but sometimes all you need is your own company.

Without other people to consider, you're free to explore your own ideas and make up interesting stories, you can invent games and get on with your own projects.

Being able to have a great time on your own is a special skill. It's not that you don't like others, it's just that you really want to explore all the good things going on in your own mind.

Lonely

You might feel like you're all alone, with no friends. You wish someone could understand, right now. The odd thing about loneliness is that it doesn't really have anything to do with *how many* people are around you. There might be lots of people around you all the time, but you can still feel alone because they don't seem to understand you.

They're not interested in the things that excite you. Sometimes when they laugh, you don't actually think it's very funny. They want to talk about things you don't care about.

Feeling lonely can be frustrating. You want friends who you share a connection with, but you can't find them just at the moment.

School is very strange. You spend a lot of time with maybe twenty people your age. But there are billions of people on planet Earth and you've met hardly any of them so far. There are plenty of people out there who you could get on with very well.

Being lonely doesn't mean there's anything wrong with you. It just means you're looking for *really* good friends. A good way to do this is to find out what other people enjoy. You can find small connections with people, such as a love of dogs or drawing, which might help you make new friends who are more like you.

Curious

What's it like to be a butterfly? It's a great question. And there are so many others: what was there before the universe began? What would happen if absolutely everyone in the world jumped up and down at the same time? What's it like being a parent? Why are some people mean? What was it like being alive a long time ago? Why is money important?

The great thing about being curious is that you can take your time finding out. Your brain tries out lots of different possibilities. Maybe you'll find the answer in a book or online, or maybe no one can ever know. That's OK, it's just fun thinking about these things.

Curiosity is good because it means that you care about the world around you and want to understand it. It's a valuable feeling because it makes you want to learn new things.

Confused

People actually walk on the moon? That's crazy! Sometimes you feel like this. Things happen that just don't make sense to you.

But being confused isn't silly. A lot of things really are truly confusing. You might have two best friends and they're both really great but they don't like each other. Or your parents got you exactly what you wanted for your birthday but you don't feel as happy as you thought you would. Or you have to choose a drink when you don't know which one you want.

Life is genuinely confusing and this feeling is a very intelligent response.

Amazed

Something is wonderful and it makes you feel wonderful, too. The sunset, looking up at the stars, a plane taking off, a spider spinning a web ... many things are exciting in a special way. They make you feel small because they're so huge or powerful or beautiful and you (or any person) don't seem to matter compared to them. But because you're excited, you feel swept up in what you see, and your imagination gets very big.

It's a very important kind of feeling. Not a lot of adults talk about it, which is a pity. If you want to give an adult a big surprise, just tell them you were 'amazed' by a lightning storm!

It doesn't mean the lightning hit you; it means a big feeling hit you. It doesn't hurt, though. It's lovely.

Happy

Feeling happy – that's the best. It's when you can't stop smiling and it feels like the sun is shining inside your brain.

What is it that actually makes you happy though? It's a really good question, but the answer can be unexpected. If you see an advert, you might think, 'If I get this new thing, I'll be so happy.' But maybe the really happy times are when you play hide-and-seek with your cousins or you have an interesting idea or you're nice to someone who's lonely and make a new friend. You can feel happy just waking up on a lovely sunny morning.

You can't be happy all the time, but that's OK. When you're feeling sad or lonely, or worried or hurt, you can do some of the things that make you feel happy, like playing hide-and-seek. You might find yourself feeling better.

And one last thing ...
What are they feeling?

You might be surprised by the interesting feelings other people have. This book has been all about your feelings. You feel lots of different things and other people might not know what they are – unless you tell them. But that means something very important: if *they* don't know what *you're* really feeling, then sometimes *you* won't know what *they're* really feeling either.

There are so many different people in the world. Why not use what you know about your feelings to imagine what other people might be feeling?

But bear in mind – how they feel might be different from how they behave! Your feelings make *you* interesting. And other people's feelings make *them* interesting, too.

ISBN: 978-1-912891-24-5

£15.00 | $19.99

An Emotional Menagerie

Feelings from A to Z

An imaginative and engaging exploration of childhood emotions through poetry and evocative illustrations.

Emotions are like animals:
No two are quite the same.
Some are gentle; others, fierce;
And some are hard to tame.

Children experience all sorts of emotions, sometimes going through several very different ones before breakfast. Yet they can struggle to put these feelings into words. An inability to understand and communicate their moods can lead to 'bad' behaviour, deep frustration and a whole host of difficulties further down the line.

An Emotional Menagerie is an emotional glossary for children. A book of 26 rhyming poems, arranged alphabetically, that bring our feelings to life – Anger, Boredom, Curiosity, Dreaminess, Embarrassment, Fear, Guilt, and more.

Filled with wise, therapeutic advice and brought to life through musical language and beautiful illustrations, *An Emotional Menagerie* is an imaginative and universally appealing way of increasing emotional literacy.

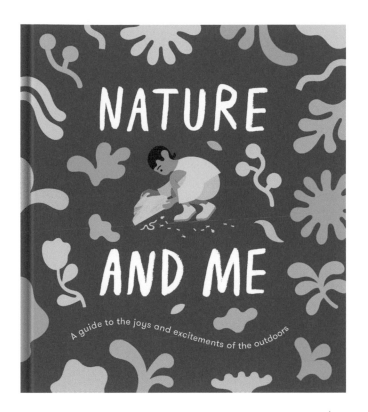

ISBN: 978-1-912891-31-3

£15.00 | $19.99

Nature and Me

A guide to the joys and excitements of the outdoors

An essential guide to encourage children to explore, enjoy and benefit from the natural world around them.

Children are constantly being told how important nature is and that natural things are good for them. But it's still often hard for them to know why nature might actually be fun, uplifting, consoling – and a real friend for them.

This is a book about how nature can touch us all and help us with our lives (especially when we might be feeling bored, sad or lonely). We learn about the ways in which we can come to love and be inspired by various examples from nature, such as:

- a giant anteater
- a view of the Alps
- a flatfish
- the night sky
- an okapi
- a cuddle with a favourite puppy

In this book, we aren't just lectured to about nature, we are taught to love and connect with it – through beautiful illustrations and a tone that's encouraging, warm and easy for children, and their favourite adults, to relate to.

To join The School of Life community and find out more, scan below:

The School of Life publishes a range of books on essential topics in psychological and emotional life, including relationships, parenting, friendship, careers and fulfilment. The aim is always to help us to understand ourselves better – and thereby to grow calmer, less confused and more purposeful. Discover our full range of titles, including books for children, here:
www.theschooloflife.com/books

The School of Life also offers a comprehensive therapy service, which complements, and draws upon, our published works:
www.theschooloflife.com/therapy

www.theschooloflife.com